As the Flow Goes

Goes

A compilation of my Thoughts and Poetry

Kia Flow

As The Flow Goes: *A compilation of my thoughts and poetry*

Copyright © 2017 Takia "Kia Flow" Dickens
www.KiaFlow.com

Cover Design by **Capture Life Productions**
Author Photo by **Inkera Oshun**

Logo Design by **Shane Manier**

ISBN: 978-1975987299

Printed in the United States of America

Contents of this book

Introduction
6

Happy Times
9

Sing in Royal Love
14

Little Black Dress
18

I don't watch the News
21

Intuitive Desire
27

Game Show of Love
31

Silly
37

Haiku Poems
42

Where Would I be
43

A Day in the Life
47

A Work in Progress
51

A Conversation on Racism
54

This Dance
59

The Food Piece
63

Obsession
69

Addiction
73

Bring those days back
77

The Nerd
83

A Love of Your Own
89

Spit
95

A Fifth of Loyalty
101

Do You Know Her?
107

Inspirational Piece
114

I dedicate this book to my grandma.

Thank you for believing in me and never leaving me.

Lou Eva

5/27/45 – 12/07/12

Introduction

I've traveled a few years with my book in tow and didn't even know. I was waiting for a great escape to a faraway place with rusty water and smoky air for days. Wine glass and trees, I thought, when I wrote my book I'd be prepared. I was completely unaware that I was preparing myself for the desires lingering in my thoughts daily, plaguing my sleep, toying with my breath. I thought I had to plan the book release and set deadlines in order to find the time to free my mind to paper pages. Future finger aches and grammar mistakes, spell check on standby, I thought it took time. But I didn't realize that time was on my side and in my pocket, purse, hand or charger my book was there. Waiting for my attention. Waiting for my acknowledgment of its existence. And I didn't even know. But just as my flow goes I have to go with it. I finally have many of my poetry and thoughts formatted to the standards of the "professional book people" and I'm grateful.

So I want to thank you for opening these pages. Hopefully something you read allows you to think differently about anything and nothing in particular. I'd like to think of myself as a different type of individual and because of that I have provided a few back stories and commentary to some of my poetry. Although the interpretation of the reader is appreciated, I'd like to clear or eliminate any wonder and provide insight that the piece won't always provide because of the messages' primary focus. Also some of my material has offensive language. Daddy I apologize in advance! I wanted to give you my thoughts and views how I think and view them. I love everyone. I do I do I do. Once again thank you for reading and I hope you enjoy.

Now let's go with The Flow...

And the saying goes "every dog has it's day". I can't say I know the true meaning of that phrase but to me the meaning says that the time will always come where reality will encounter accountability and as a result judgement and consequence are sure to follow. Eventually ending in fatality. That is the ultimate "dog's day". I feel that every time I see a dead dog on the highway. But to tie that into my first piece - which is not about dead dogs, I felt I had reached my "day" in poetry and contemplated letting it all go. My reality at the time was too much for me to juggle with art so I backed away completely. Although I partly felt it was necessary. I believe this piece sprouted hands, pulled me up off the ground, dusted me off and pushed me into my first poetry slam in over a year. This piece got me my first winners circle slot. This piece comforts me whenever doubt appears.

Happy Times

Hollowed beginnings with countless miraculous endings

Wavering on which direction to explore

Happy times no more

She gets lost in thoughts of what could have been

Darkness wraps its fingers around her optimism

Choking infinite possibilities into dust

Happy times no more

Once there lived a giggling child of success

With shiny lights of stability draped around her neck like

diamonds and candy

Hiding and seeking life in her smile

She was ready for whatever came next

Happy times no more

Haven't been seen in days, and it's only a matter of time

before peace and serenity dissipate

In her buried memories next to the oak tree.

Worry plagues her psyche

As She falls to her knees

Feeling the pressure from the whispers

Then doubt begins to enter her well-built castle

Her foundation begins to crumble and stones do break

bones.

Plus she believes she's losing layer after layer of

security

But eventually she understands that she will have to

break free

Cuz she wants those happy times to visit like

grandparents on Christmas eve

She wants to live gratis of care like those days as an

adolescent

When the weights on her shoulder were easily lifted with

a kiss and ice cream.

Now she's responsible for her actions

And the only mile she can journey is the one she created.

Abandoned out of fear of failure

But She knows the way.

Songs deeper than the drinking gourd live embedded in

her DNA

She knows the way

She knows how to plant the seed, and water the seed,

and watch it grow

She's the sunlight of life.

The fire in her eyes provides warmth to lost souls

Bold she was born and Bold she will die

Because the fire in those eyes it's what fuels those happy

times.

Determined and dipped in armor fit for a queen.

She picked herself up off the cold damp soil seeping

through the cracks of her foundation

And Let her light shine

Left darkness and pessimism behind.

Found love in her bloodline and... bled.

Bled so souls could be fed

Became at ease with the decisions made.

For all may not be the ones to keep her saved, but there's

a lesson in battle.

And she knew she was not in this war alone.

So she continued to use the fire in her eyes, and your

eyes as her guiding light to continue to press on.

Sing in Royal Love

Time after time I wrack my brain with thoughts of being too expecting.

Expecting that perfect treatment I used to hear about in love songs of yesterday.

But maybe I need to listen to the lyrics of today to decipher what love I will receive before expecting you to treat me like the queen you all love to call us women these days.

Seems to be yet another sacred title washed away with new-age meanings of nothing.

You call me your queen and expect me to treat you with royalty.

Wanting me to be that lady in the street, freak in the sheets, tight, wet, stroker, but instead of my king before me stands a joker.

Not the trump card type of playa but a chump scared type of busta.

I try to give you the benefit of the doubt because I know how men hate to be compared to the next.

I be that lady you require and the freak you desire along with other characteristics only God could have blessed.

And you still show me nothing different.

You get on my back and attempt to make me feel less of a woman,

trying to force in me that what I see is only imaginary.

That I am over dramatic in the fact that I compare you to the average.

You use your words to try and make me see that you are different than he, but your actions leave before they had a chance to enter, because you think simple and feel that you're keeping it real by letting me know what you need up front.

Not realizing that I am an intuitive woman and better beginnings I help create and launch

But before I submit and be that vessel to ALL your innermost wants and desires, I need your trust to take me to areas far greater than higher,

I need you to secure me emotionally and protect me mentally and I know there's an attraction but what you see between my legs is only a fraction of the dynamics of this black dynamic creation. For one day these golden gates I'm sure you'll grace.

Mr. be polite for once without putting up a front because most times it's about what we need not what we want.

I can give you love and so much more. I see your heart and lack of direction, PLUS I noticed your erection!

Darling, baby love won't you come see about me and our chemistry. It sits right before thee.

I just need you to clear your mind from the pollution of misguided teachings, I promise you I'm not preaching, I'm just thinking of ways to get this union on track.

True love and understanding is obviously something we both lack.

Let's tune out the world and its songs and create our own lyrics for each other.

Because after all a King and Queen were mean to serenade one another.

Little Black Dress

Little black dress, oh how you make me sick

You knew I specifically picked you for tonight's event

I tried you on and wondered how many numbers would I

get

But I guess you said to yourself "I got something for this

bitch"

Because no... soon as I put you on and headed out the

door, your cheap ass split.

You had me thinking to myself "That's what my fat ass

get"

Man... I walked out the store smiling from ear to ear cuz

I knew I had just caught a lick.

But see I'm a woman about mine and I'm grown enough

to admit

That I knew you were 2 dress sizes too small so it was

gonna be a tight fit.

18

But you see you were the last one on the clearance rack

so I knew you were the right pick.

And as for the love handles and jelly rolls, oh the body

magic would hide it.

You added fullness to my breast and made my ass look

super thick

And although you were plain, the right shoes and

accessories would do the trick.

I even wore black thongs so you wouldn't see my

underwear print.

But I guess you thought you ended my night pretty

quick.

You thought that you would spoil my fun by unraveling

your sewn up slits.

You thought that you would rob me of night of

happiness with your unexplained wits.

But ha ha no no! To the sewing machine we go because

this rip... I could fix.

You will not rob me of a chance at having a wonderful

night of bliss.

Oh little black dress, oh how you thought you were slick.

But you fucked up when you ran across the eye of this,

bargain shopping, accessorizing, sewing machine having

chick!

I Don't Watch the News

I'm sorry but I don't watch the news.

The heart wrenching sometimes divesting stories give me the blues. So I choose to change the channel. Hoping that happiness will channel through the radio frequencies and put my mind at ease, when I switch the screen.

I'm sorry but I don't watch the news.

The videos of yellow tape have been permanently burned in my brain.

Somehow becoming the new light of rain, oh how my eyes strain to see beyond the crime scene barrier. Only to see stretchers and carriers, rushing innocent lives to safety.

But no one is safe see.

Because bullets have no name.

I'm sorry but I don't watch the news.

Hearing voices, but only seeing shirts and hands of those too afraid to show their faces.

21

Some choosing to erase the knowledge known but unknown, because all they want to do is journey on, and live to see another day.

Praying their life away, in hopes that their life will stay.

Loud mumbles rumble like thunder under these wicked streets.

The truth buried too deep to seep through the concrete, so no voices speak.

I'm sorry but I don't watch the news.

There have been several times when I have walked out my front door improperly dressed for the weather.

Miniskirts worn in snow storms and turtlenecks worn through heat waves because I didn't check with the weatherman.

Although I wanted to wait on the weatherman, the today's top story about a man beating an elderly man made me turn to PBS.

So now I'm improperly dressed because of this mess.

Too lazy to go get a 9 to 5 so they rob and take lives for chump change.

Don't it seem strange that these stations thrive off these stories to boost their ratings.

I'm sorry but I don't watch the news.

I missed the good news on the schools with the highest marks.

And I missed the news about the location of the new Super Walmart.

I missed the news on Housewives tips on shopping smart, and I missed the news on what brands of wines are good for the heart because, I heard at work today that a child killed another child because he lost a game of football.

So now I'm home not trying to watch channel 4, 12 or 47, 30 at all.

Because I know I'll see tears of mothers crying out to the Lord for answers.

And no I didn't know there was a breakthrough in the cure for cancer, because I don't watch the news.

I didn't see the local town's High school player of the week, and I'm assuming no one has stomped coach yet.

I didn't know that the adoption centers were overcrowded with pets or that they posted an address on how to mail get well letters to disabled war vets.

You know I got sick from eating at a restaurant that apparently scored an F and speaking of food does that one news channel still show that gray haired chef?

I heard they showed a segment on fruits that were bad for your health, but I guess I will never know because I don't watch the news. I don't watch the news because I hate the feeling I get when I hear bad news.

….Like finding out that one of your classmates was shot dead through her front door while she sat on the couch.

...Or finding out a classmate got killed because she visited the wrong house.

...Or seeing a 19 year old get stabbed in the neck in front of a beauty supply store or seeing that a young man was gunned down as he walked out his front door.

It's like my brain got fed up and said I can't take it no more.

Why must you watch this nonsense for? It seems to be only a TV show of murders galore.

I'm sorry but I don't watch the news.

I feel that Wheel of Fortune is a lot more appealing than the Wheel of Justice,

Because based on the events that happen in today's society I question validity of this thing we call justice.

And I ain't saying all the segments are bad, or that I am boycotting the finely tuned broadcast.

But I personally find it hard to get past the breathtaking stories viewed en masse. I'm sorry but I don't watch the news.

And I'm only expressing my personal opinion on why I

don't watch the news.

I'll just let you watch it and I get my info from you.

And there may be a time or two where my attention is glued to the stories shown on the tube, but those are few far and between.

And maybe the decrease of violence will redeem my faith in the local stories of today.

But as of right now, let me be the 1st to say and apologize, but I'm sorry. I just don't watch the news!

Intuitive Desire

My mind is clear in the midst of my confusion.

But you are the one I am pursuing and at any cost am I

willing to reach you.

I see people flocking and hoping to touch you and see

what it feels like.

Hoping to carry you one day on their arms and flaunt.

Caught in a daze by the glamour it's such a cliché you

are.

Anticipating your promises of a better tomorrow.

You come in different flavors to savor.

Once you're captured the end result is so sweet.

Some people travel months and miles to just be in your

presence.

Hoping that you would at least brush up against them.

A lot of people are in debt just to try to obtain you.

You drive a hard bargain for some.

Others it's just pure luck (if there's a such thing)

You're like a diamond in the rough

Fatality can also be your name.

With no shame a bitch can be put out like a light if they

step in the way of getting to you.

It's like you're a force to be reckoned with.

But still I am drawn to you.

Why can't I get you off my mind.

What do I need from you.

My mind is clear in the midst of my confusion, but how

can I ease the pain of your essence.

I want to have you so bad that I can't breathe right.

My blinks hurt because I'm scared you will waltz past

with the speed of light.

Where the fuck is my appetite.

You make some people look so pretty, I want all of that

Come on man, when is my day gone come.

It's been said that no good deed goes unpunished.

Is this my punishment? Because I know I have done a lot of good deeds in my time.

Promises are broken in order to wait on your possible arrival.

Just faking the part won't do.

I want to have the real you, in full force.

And I know I can't come half stepping when I get you.

I know I have to pay the cost to be the boss.

You offer me things no man can ever give me.

I'm so jealous when I see others with you.

My mind is clear in the midst of my confusion, but my confusion is taking over.

Success, please say you will be mine.

Please say I can carry you on my arm and be pretty, and have fame and friends, and love.

Please say that with you, I will find happiness, and will go to heaven.

Please say that I will have kids, and a dog that will obey

my every command.

Please say that my car will never be on E again, and all

my clothes will fit perfectly.

My mind is clear in the midst of my confusion, but what

is it that I am really pursuing?

Game Show of Love

Girl feeling dude and dude feeling girl.

Girl and dude start kickin it.

Dude is hella nice to girl and girl be tryin to make dude happy.

Dude like what he see in girl, but he also likes what he sees in others.

Girl done started fallin for dude, but dude ain't ready to take it there.

Dude shows girl affection and attention and that's what got girl head gone.

The only way girl know how to play it cool is to put a brick wall up, but dude don't like that.

Girl tells dude that if she is affectionate then she will start falling hard for him.

Dude once again says he's not ready for all dat action.

So girl tells dude she gone have to fall back and keep it on a friend type level till he ready.

31

Dude tells her alright but don't be surprised if another girl takes her spot.

And that's where the cycle begins.

So desperately wanting a man to want us that we are willing to compete for his heart.

We have unknowingly submitted our head shots, biography and resume to "The Game Show of Love"

Constantly trying to find ways for him to make us his #1.

Sometimes putting any moral beliefs and feelings to the side in order to make a "good thing" work.

Continuously believing that stupid motto that some women recite "I'd rather have a piece of a man, than no man at all."

See in this game show of love, no one wants to be labeled **the biggest loser**.

So we conjure up all sorts of tactics and strategies to be crowned the **Survivor**. But what did you really survive?

Relying on the what ifs as if it was the only thing that made sense in our life. **This is your life**.

Some of us give our all for chump change and lint balls in return. Baby boy may be gone til Nov but you sit waiting for his return. Desperately wanting to be labeled his ride or die.

Dreading the mere thought of being labeled the **Weakest Link**.

But let's put the reality in reality check, cuz we live in the **real world**.

And in the real world there are plenty of men out there to choose from.

Have your own **Super market sweep**.

Are you gonna like all the products on the shelves? Probably not. But at least you know you can browse, bargain and barter.

No need to play **Let's make a deal** or **deal or no deal** unless he's willing to seal the deal… with you.

Stop jumping and climbing to be at the top of his **Pyramid**, cuz little do you know it or not but girl you are the pyramid. If you can't be his # only don't settle for being #1, because we all know that if there is a 1 then there's a 2 or 3 or 4 shall I continue?

You possess the key to unlock that mystery door.

And no this is not a male bashing poem, because truth be told ma, he done laid his cards out for ya. He done rolled the dice and passed go about 3 times, while you still trying to get outta jail.

But when it's all said and done, if he can't see your worth and your mental **wheel of fortune**, you need to drop dude like a **plinko** chip.

It doesn't take a hundred surveyed people for you to know that you deserve that ace of high status.

And if a **5th grader** is smart enough to know that if lil Timmy is giving jolly ranchers to other girls on the playground, that the gift is not as special as she thought, what the hell is clouding your perception?

I know you're desperately looking for that **Love Connection**, but when are you gonna stop wanting to be the **5th Wheel**?

Tell me this, what are you going to do when or if he **gongs** your ass during your performance?

Oh now you gonna be bitter huh?

Trust me I know how it feels to **play to win**, but you can never spin the wheel on that dollar. And I know you hate when you have placed your wager and the next chick bids a dollar over and wins the spot light.

We need to learn how to start playing it cool, and I ain't saying drop dude, but don't **Boggle** your brain over why or why not just do you. And if push comes to shove you may have to let him go. Cuz there's no need to sell your soul for a love that may never show or grow. We all wanna be a **millionaire**, but **don't forget the lyrics** to that song in your heart. The lyrics that say: It's not right but it's ok. I'm gonna make it anyway.

The Dating Game gamble and at any given time someone can have a **Change of Heart**. Just know that in a real relationship it only Takes Two to make a thing go right. If he can't leave the other bachelorettes out, then you really don't need him. Don't go around starting mess with the other women to get your point across. Cuz lord knows I hate when women try to **Gladiator** it out. Don't put your life and values in **Jeopardy** for what or who you think is the **Eligible Bachelor**. Show him that he is actually missing a good thing if he loses you. Girl tell him he should be able to taste your **flavor of Love** without even placing his lips on you.

A lot of our **Downfalls** are either chasing men or trying to change them. Don't do either cuz when the chips have been thrown in and the books have been bided you may think you're **Set for Life**. But what did you risk or give up to obtain it.

Silly

You knew all the right words to say. How to say them, when to say them, and how you would smell or the pitch in your voice when you spoke them.

You knew that the thicker and mellower your tone became, my heart would ooze with pleasure and excitement from your premeditated lyrics... of deceit.

You knew that the warmth of your grasp would sizzle my desire to want to feel, that sensation in this spot, and that place or that area.

You knew that your eyes possessed some type of magnetic force that would trample any sense of doubt that lingered in my spirit. So powerful that if I swallowed, I would feel your force streaming through my bloodline, saturating my tissue, coating my linings and swishing through my stomach acid, patiently waiting.

Waiting for me to give in. Waiting for me to fall in love

with your actions, not your being.

You knew that I liked direct eye contact... Especially when you did that, and tasted that.

You gazed into my soul, and found the perfect spot to nest, and slowly as you sucked... on... it... you sucked that life out of me.

It's like instantly I was no longer me. That climax made me lose my will to think womanly. And right then and there you knew you had me. You were like a mosquito that would suck the blood out but input poison. Your poison was your control.

I became weak off your poison, and you knew it.

So you would wrap your arms around my anatomy, and place a kiss in the right spot, sorta like your stamp of approval.

Mission accomplished. I got her where I want her.

My vulnerability was now your playground, and you had a fuckin ball..

You knew that if you entered me with exact concentration and depth, that my inner most thoughts and feelings would seep out at the mere satisfaction.

You knew that your substance was thick enough to fill every void once etched into my love. "With your cocky ass".

You drained me mentally with every drawback of you, but filled me with false hope with every thrust.

Somehow I thought you cared, and wanted more of me, but you wanted more from me. And you wouldn't stop until you had me totally.

You deposited your spirit in me and I was instantly confused. An active comatose patient is what I was, in a vegetative state with full use of my body.

Mortified at even the slightest thought of losing you. Tricked into thinking you were chosen for me. Somehow it was destiny that you and me were laying skin to skin, flesh to flesh, ashes to ashes, chest to chest.

What I just briefly described is nothing short of the ordinary. It's when you are silly mad in love with someone, but the signs are all there that show you, that this person means you no good. But our flesh wants what it wants, and sometimes at any cost. What price are you willing to pay? We confuse brief satisfaction with love. I can only speak from a woman's point of view, but I know men go through it to. Those people who have gone through it, sometimes more than once, can feel me on this. Those of you who may go through this might be able to become a little more mindful and be able to decipher bull shit from meaningful love. Those of you who will go through this, just hold on and stay prayed up and just know that everyone is allowed one time to be stupid for love, but let's not make it habit. Because I'd rather be a lonely but happy mother f***er than a fool for a nigga any day. Never again my friend.

Because I know my self-worth. And I know what I have to offer, and nigga if you can't see that, then you obviously have the problem.

Haiku Poems

<u>Team Natural</u>

Naturally Me

Who I've always strived to be

Ain't shaving my legs

<u>Date Dot Com</u>

Want what they can't have

Ignore those who want them most

Single forever

<u>Norman</u>

He's strumming my pain

I felt all flushed with fever

Killing me softly

Where Would I be...

I wonder where would I be if my booty was bigger.

Would I be the apple of someone's eye or just another gold digger.

Would I have the hottest whip and stay looking ever so clean.

Or would I be some city's "baddest" stripper, strippin to get her way on the front cover of a men's magazine.

If I walked into a room would the men all pause.

Or would I instantly be judged with no reason, fact or cause.

If I was 5 with a big ass would the boys write me cute lil do you like me notes.

Or would the girls tease and fight me, because I'm the center of all their jokes.

I wonder where would I be if my booty was bigger.

Would I be labeled a beautiful chocolate curvy woman,

or just another big booty nigger.

If I walked into an interview, would I be a shoo in for the position.

Or would my salary be contingent upon the amount of my tricks proposition.

If I was 17 with a big ass would I be asked to the prom and provided a corsage.

Or would I be someone's big booty jump off for a teenage ménage.

If I got pulled over for speeding would the police let me go with ease.

Or could the only way I get off scot-free is by blessing him while down on my knees.

I wonder where would I be if my booty was bigger.

Would I be glorified and praised or would I be criticized about my voluptuous figure.

Would he cherish and love me and want nothing more than to marry me.

Or would he love me and leave me, for the next phat ass he sees.

Would I be CEO of a Fortune 500

Or would I be backseat action for every nigga I see driving a 300.

If I hailed down a taxi would they stop with a haste.

If I had a basket full of groceries would he still let me take his place.

If I was at the bar alone would he buy me a drink.

Hell would he buy the whole bar out, without even a blink

Would my friend not want me around her man cuz she knows he will stare.

Would he crash his whip because the site of my ass made his vision impaired.

Would he be able to handle all this ass when I'm throwin it back.

Would it ripple like a tidal wave with the gentlest smack.

Or would my life be a living hell, always getting disrespected.

Stereotyped, talked about and always rejected.

Would my landlord give me a 30 day eviction cuz I wouldn't give up the goods.

Would my nickname be *Loose Booty Judy* dubbed by all the cats in the hood.

Would my kids be ashamed of me when came up to their school.

Would I continue to lose in love because I'm the one that always plays the fool.

Would my life be easy or would I have it hard.

Would having a phat ass leave me emotionally scarred?

These are just pure assumptions or what I figure on where I would be if my booty was bigger.

Now don't get me or my booty "twisted" because we get along just fine!

This poem is dedicated to my momma! For some reason she cries laughing EVERY SINGLE TIME I recite this for her.

A Day in the Life

I was chillin home alone with nothing to do, So I called **Whitney Houston** to hear some good news. I said Whitney wassup make it do what it do! But she kept talking about how she's **Saving all her love** for some gyrating, pelvis shaking, twisted mouth fool.

So I got my shit together and was headed out the do', until I got an instant message from my boy **Peabo**. He was rappin bout how he was **So Into me** and couldn't stop callin my name, I said I'm also into you as long as you don't **Stop the Rain.**

Now **Kanye** told me I wasn't no **gold digger** so don't

think I'm wrong, but he da one dat stepped up to me talking about his money was oh so long.

So now I'm rollin in my whip on a nothing ass day, when I hear a smooth cut by the late **Marvin Gaye**, now I kinda understood what this guy was feeling. Cuz all he really wanted was some **Sexual Healing.**

Pulled up at the Hot Wok where they are known to be feisty, that's when I got a collect call from my boy **Ronald Isley**. He talking about breaking out of prison cuz he really couldn't stand it. Said his brothers gone bust him out and they're going to take a **Voyage to Atlantis**.

Now this dude was buggin, I told him I'll talk to him later, and as I was walkin out da restaurant in walks **Anita Baker.** I said **No One in the World** has a voice like you, she said well thank you **Angel**, and God bless you boo.

So I went to the Walmart parking lot to eat my food, when I heard a loud bang behind my Lexus coupe. I got out my car to see what was the deal, when low and behold **Stevie Wonder** done ran into the back of **Johnnie Gill. My My My** was all I could say, but Mr Stevie Wonder was for some odd reason singing **Happy Birthday**.

I didn't want to be a witness so I tried to flee the scene, but before I could put the key in the ignition, I see my nosey neighbor. **Rev Al Green**. Now although he was nosey, he was an alright kinda fella, so as the police came up I said **Let's stay together**, and tell them what happened so I can get out this mess. He nodded and agreed and started singing **Love and Happiness.**

After all of that was over man I left with haste. That was too much drama in one setting and I needed some space. As I'm heading back home I saw a smile I couldn't erase, he was standing at the bus stop with a vase and some mace. I asked him for his name and if he was sure he was safe, he said my name's **Babyface** and I'll be safe with this mace. I said alright take it easy with the slickest of grins, he said baby hold up **When can I see you again?**

I quickly sped off cuz dude was kinda creepy, plus my topsy turvy day had your girl kinda sleepy. From collect calls and car accidents, to grit burned pastors, I had to hurry and get my thoughts together amongst all the laughter. Thanks for listening to my silly poem, hope it brought you some delight, Thanks for listening to my crazy behind journey or what I like to call A Day in the

Life!

I remember when I wrote this piece. It was just a thought when I wrote it, or shall I say a caption on Instagram. I was in a deep and heavy place and time in my life and was eagerly fighting to rise. I wrote this piece to have understanding that I am a work in progress and feelings I possessed in the past may not still be present today because of growth and evolution. I ask that people recognize that growth and encourage for the greatness that is in store.

A Work in Progress

The pressure is thick

Because so much has been given to me, much more is required of me, however sometimes I'm not sure what they want from me.

I sit here thinking of my next move, the best move, not caring what the rest do.

51

Hoping to be more stress proof there's a test due that I

never studied for, not even sure if I'm going to pass this

course,

But my brain and feet work simultaneously to never

stand still and accept defeat.

Better times and understanding is what I seek.

Wondering internally

Why did I pick all the bad habits.

Finding loopholes and new tactics to calm my madness.

I'm a strong woman weakened with grief and grudge,

eyes change directions quickly when I realize there's

nothing in it for me showing no love.

But I do have a heart, and although it is emotionally

scarred I try to do right by it and write through it.

I long to be better, better than I was yesterday and

tomorrow.

Ignoring the sorrow running out my cup sometimes I lay

stuck in my head searching for answers

And when I find none I begin to justify

Ignoring the possible whys as to why I don't try a little

harder to break away from the curses birthed in me

living intensely...

I mean I just want to be free.

So as I continue to work on me all I want y'all to see is

the woman I've grown to be

Because I'm a work in progress.

My Libra scales often cause me to weigh out options most closed-minded individuals wouldn't give a second thought to. My blackness however causes me to weigh out my true feelings with what makes others comfortable. As a result I remain conflicted most times and confused others.

My thoughts on Racism

How do I feel?

Vulnerable.

Because I'm open to hoping that our purpose will show its face.

Open because I'm able to admit that most time these days I fear I'll never know,

I was taught to serve my purpose but I get weary with each day because what if that time will never appear.

All because of someone's fear.

So I sit

And think of ways to survive the war, getting blazed to

keep my mind away from the pain I see

Daily

Confused because I don't know what set the fuse but I

refuse to believe that this is the end.

That this is the way we are carried out of this world,

because I've heard the stories. And seen remnants of our

history. The golden and warm or deep and brown kings

and queens. The tribes and their rituals. The songs and

the dance ring low and loud in my soul and I refuse to

believe that it is our time to go.

Yet I still don't know. How not to be confused in times

like these.

How to be in times like these.

Do I still trust in times like these.

Do I still love in times like these.

Constantly praying and listening out for those soft

voices, that all give direction.

But where's our protection, I constantly reflect and

I never forget those who fought this fight before me

Stood tall and proud for freedom and liberty.

They put that fight in me.

They've enlightened me

But how do I be

When my freedom to breathe is taken from me

Is it wrong that we demand justice and peace?

Dismissing our cries from the backlash of corruption and

greed.

Refusing to die quiet, so we riot because it was your

personal need to be more than human.

But the world is dying.

Every day is a battle somewhere while many of us think

it's all good over here..

And the media has me buggin.

So many point of views being spewed most times have

me not sure of what to think.

I had to take a step back.

Had my mind traveling places it didn't need to be at.

Wondering do I need to get prepared.

Angry because I'm not already.

Realizing that it ain't a game.

Not knowing which step to take first.

Still wanting to be the voice of reason, but the shots

people who look like me have taken has my heart

bleeding.

And the only thing I can hear among the whispers is

Seclusion and **preparation**.

But I'm trying to better myself.

Isolation

But how can I give my brothers and sisters help

Peace and **Serenity**

But how will my light shine.

Freedom for **eternity**.

57

And this fight is deeper than anything my eyes probably

will ever see. Well regardless of which direction I take...

I just hope you remember me.

No Justice No Peace

I woke up out of my sleep to write this piece. Never had that happened to me. A few weeks after writing this piece a song came on the radio that brought new meaning to this poem. Let the Music Play by Shannon has been my one of my favorites since forever. It was released in 1985 the year I was born and my mother had the song on vinyl. I asked if she remembered playing it while pregnant with me and she said yes.

This Dance

I found myself drifting in and out a state of confusion after our encounter on the dance floor went sourly silent or silently sour.

Confused in the feelings from my ways or the way I was feeling because I assumed you read my rhythm.

I assumed that when you swung my way, your heart tuned in to what my hips had to say or at least your mind.

I assumed that your 2 step combined with mine and we held deep conversations hearing every word even with 808s blazing.

The boom created a groove that caused our mid sections to move to the same tune.

I assumed that you understood the slight separation of my thighs along with the passion in my eyes was language for acceptance and comfort-ability.

That beyond this dance floor you could always be comfortable with me.

The accent in my melody allowed you to get free.

I assume that the build of the beat would bring you closer to me.

Through my tempo I assumed you knew me.

But somehow the music stopped.

Along with rays in our future étoilé you let the movement drop and you stopped dancing.

Let go of my hand and found another prima to pose with

your calculated pace of persecution.

I assumed you knew this dance was for you.

My thoughts tiptoed back to the bridge.

When I placed my hand in yours as I turned.

Your hand at the small of my back guiding me into your aura made my spirit yearn.

Alluding that you wanted more of this moment.

I assumed my arch is what you wanted.

I assumed that this dance would last for an eternity.

But you let go of me.

Let go of the possibilities of we

You slid away and left your scent on my sweat, your lingering energy caressed my chest.

Left my groove upset.

I assumed you knew that this dance was for you.

But I'm the fool.

Round here shucking and jiving to impress you.

Even with your two left feet.

I felt your salsa/merengue combination was created for me.

That's my comedic relief.

To the situation you left for me.

But I guess I'll rock and shake,

Summonsing the DJ to let the music play

Standing in the spotlight so the right one can notice me

And hopefully his heart is opened to the blues in my left and the junk in my back.

Hopefully he doesn't lack the concentration and understanding of romance with an 8 count of life.

That I'd cherish his moonlight for one night in ecstasy's pastime paradise.

Soon as the music stops, once out of his trance, he'd then come too.

And when he'd ask where I got my dance moves from, I'd simply say.

Honey, I assumed you knew this dance was just for you.

The Food Piece

Big Mac a little cheese.

Quarter-Pounder, French Fries.

Icy Cola, Milk Shake, Sundae and an Apple Pie.

My oh my how those fries shape my thighs.

And the Apple pies of my eyes.

Taste buds dripping with moistened saliva of sodium, starch, and sugar anticipation.

The creation of the drive thru makes me proud to be an American.

I can get a delicious feast made my way in under 4 minutes. All while listening to some rapper, fixing my makeup and checkin my Facebook statuses.

Likes.

Oh how I love chewing chicken chalupas with the cheese coating the corners of my crescent mooned mouth.

Call me Freddy cuz I'm ready for some meatballs and spaghetti and I ain't being petty but can you sprinkle me some extra Parmesan cheese please.

And yes I got my healthy side of salad. Wit diced ham, bacon bits, half a gallon of ranch, cheddar cheese, bleu cheese, eggs, onions, olives, turkey, and chicken.

I think I'm fixin to have a fit if they don't hurry up with my 7 layer triple chocolate delight cake with chocolate syrup drizzled on the plate.

For Pete's sake, how many cows does it take to make a triple whopper.

Biting into the flame broiled-ness, wiping the tomato and mayonnaise mixture off my chin.

I grin with complete satisfaction.

Gimme my Ritalin because I'm about to go bonkers if I don't get my Chitterlings mixed with Hog Maws or what about a Chili Slaw Dog.

They think I'm phony cuz I like pizza pepper pepperoni'd out! I hate sauerkraut, but it looks so good on a sausage dog with extra mustard.

The kiss of a creamy custard tickles my sugar rush and crushes the bud that tastes my tongue.

Yummy yum yum can I have some of your baby backs before I have an attack, and Imma wash it down with a 6 pack of Sunkist that is. Cuz I do I do I do ooo Love soda pop.

I'll make it drop for a dollop of whip cream on top.

On top of what?

On top of that strawberry, double fudge berry, cherry Sundae that's what.

All the sweetness goes to my gut, or maybe my butt, but ahh its all good.

Because he loves them love handles.

But tell me, can he handle rushing me to the emergency room once a week because my breath stops while I sleep?

My Dr. told me that the reason why my menstruation ain't regulating is because the types of food I'm intaking.

I may be cute but I tell ya what ain't cute. A 25 year old strapped to a dialysis machine, because my renal system done failed me due to diabetes which in my family is hereditary. Micky D's please stop callin my name.

I swear the value menus are a curse.

They have the right amount of fulfillment for the $3.21 I have in my pockets.

But they are clogging my blood sockets or arteries making strokes more like a reality and not a swimming technique.

But it seems as if my life is not complete without a tasty treat.

It's unique how the high fructose corn syrup if taken in moderation or not can raise a person's sugar so high that they lose limbs and go blind.

You may call me thick but inside I'm sick from all the chemicals, greases and fatty components that sit waiting to choke the living fight outta me.

The fight that tells me to drink H_2O instead of syrupy red cool aid.

The fight that tells me to pick up a celery stick instead of that sausage link.

The fight that tells me to walk off that grilled tilapia with steamed veggies instead of basking in your Salisbury steak, mashed potato rendezvous.

What is a girl to do. I'm surrounded by so many good foods.

Hell while writing this poem I was chewing on some Mike and Ikes.

Teeth getting sensitive with every bite.

But I guess I better get this thing right, before I'm forced to take an early final flight.

Trouble don't last always and neither does good health if you don't do right by it.

As much as I love the deep fried smothered pork chops, I

gotta let the little piggy cry "wee wee wee" all the way home.

No more lamb chops play along.

Imma hook up with the Jolly Green Giant and see what his talk game be bout.

Kia Flow coming to you live… Peace and I'm out!

I felt that I had been hearing too many "male bashing poems" on the poetry open mic scene and wanted to contribute something to the atmosphere that would uplift the fellas, but somewhere in my process of writing... I got bored. I decided to take the poem in a different direction...

Obsession

I wish there was a way for me to express how you make me feel.

But it seems as if that way has not been created yet.

Because, baby words and actions just won't do.

I've researched various books of chemistry, studied countless laws of attractions, surfed Wikipedia down to the 1st letter ever input and I still can't find that common bond.

That bond that has my heart sprung.

Just the aroma of your flesh sends my body racing.

I feel the changes being created every time you're near me.

Finding ways to conform to your being.

Boy you don't know what you do to me.

Hell I don't even think I know, but I know what I wanna do… to you.

You are so beautiful inside and out, I want to lick every pain stricken line from your face.

If ever you had a hard time I want to erase it with just a taste of your warm dark honey skin.

Your pieces I yearn to mend with the simplest caress of your body.

All I want to do is appreciate you from head to toe because… I think you're beautiful.

Love in its purest form there ain't nothing you can ask of me that I won't do.

Yes baby I will do anything for love plus do that.

Oh how we are the perfect match.

Oh how you are the perfect catch.

It's so sensual till it's almost an obsession.

It's amazing how you have my mind racing.

My thoughts are constantly chasing my heart beat as it paces to your rhythm.

Baby I feel like we are in sync.

But baby… I feel like you're ignoring me.

Baby don't you now that I would die for you and I can't even get you to answer my phone calls.

I've called your cell 7 times and your work 8… and I know you told me not to call your house out of respect for your wife but I'm about to dial that 7th digit and ring the alarm because I feel that you are taking me for granted. And granted I knew what the protocol was when I entered this affair but how dare you think you can enter me bare and think that morning after I took the morning after I was a closed chapter!?

I mask my fears with laughter, but my tears are choking me.

Just like this hold you have on me... Choking me. I can't breathe without you next to me, sexing me and choking me.

What is wrong with me?

I prayed to God to send me the right thing so I know you can't be wrong for me.

I just need you to pick up the phone see... I have to let you know how I feel.

But fuck it... If you won't answer the phone...

I KNOW A BITCH THAT WILL!!

And she shares your last name!

......My heart is no man's game!

... Ring... Ring... Ring...

Addiction

Addicted to the thrill.

Only time and experiences heal the yearning sensation.

Blinded by passion.

The taste of satisfaction is a thirst quencher.

Heated elements reach for ecstasy.

Comfortable with the temptations of the world.

Quivering bones hope for a Jones so strong.

Feel my inner desire. It begs for attention.

Ready to release a scent so sweet.

You're captured by my rhythm, watch as I sway.

Planning my attack on your spirit.

Sharpening your senses with my hue.

My psyche sees your intimidation and she's ready for

the kill.

Pressed for time as this urge can't wait.

Equipped with weapons of mass destruction aimed at

your soul.

You're unaware of what's in store.

Shivering at the mere thought of my wrath.

Your heart palpitates and your nerves pulsate.

Pure sensual infliction depicts my character.

Shameless and open anticipating your arrival.

Cloves of erotica enrapture our being.

Pondering on who will make the first move.

Seas of backed up emotion trample my want to hold

back.

And that's when I attack.

When the walls are too weak to withstand and the will to

be innocent is forgotten.

74

You know not what you have entered.

You thought you knew, but you haven't the slightest clue.

My love latches to you with a death grip.

You're entangled in my web of intensity.

I seep out onto you and exhale with delight.

Grinning with satisfaction.

You cling to me, like I'm your last breath.

I flutter inside and my thuds are strong.

Dizzy from your hold.

I'm undoubtedly yours, if only for this moment.

Feeding my appetite is a treat of a lifetime.

I claw into your flesh and purr at the moon.

We wrestle to the beat of our hearts.

With no care for the outside world for that moment.

For we know at any given time reality will set in and our

sins will lay heavy in our conscience.

For we know we have wronged one another.

We can never look at each other the same.

Because we belong to another.

But still you're my addiction.

Bring those days back

Sometimes I long to get back to a time when honey drippers were sweet, and life was innocent.

When red light meant stop and Mother may I was some of the best manners taught to man.

I wish I could go to a time when the little boys would play crate basketball on concrete streets.

And when yes ma'am is all you could say when getting slashed with the switch.

Back at that time when you would have your clothes laid out for the first day of school, you remember when the chair would sit in the middle of the floor, shirt hanging over the top, pants on the seat and a shoe peeking out under each leg.

A time when the night before Easter, you were sitting by a hot ass stove, with blue magic grease smeared all over your forehead and your hair sizzled like steak from a hot comb.

I miss the times when we would walk in packs home from school laughing, and teasing, laughing til the crowd dwindled down to just me walking home alone.

Whatever happened to Baby Roller blade, little Miss Makeup, Stretch Armstrong, Creepy Crawlers, and My Buddy?

Those days when kids respected their elders, and when you rode past a church you would turn ya speakers down.

A time when The Box Music channel was a po' man's BET. When the street lights came on, yo ass was in the house, and you bet not get up from that table until yo plate was clean, because children in Africa were and still are starving from sea to shining sea.

Life was so precious back when and then. Oh how I long to taste those Sprinkle Sprangles.

How could life be so angelic?

But I still can't forget about the struggles because that is what made most stronger.
Sugar water was the next best thing since sliced bread when no kool-aid was available.

And we had no shame smashing all the tiny bars of soap together to make one bar of soap in order to stay clean.

Washing dishes with soap powder or washing clothes
with dish detergent is a time I can remember

Whether the times were fun or foul, sometimes I wish
I could bring it back. I wish I could capture
those moments and replay them today.

Because today life has no value to some. We're
dropping like flies, and it just makes me wonder is
it really your time to go. Or is someone just taking that
time away.

The cries sadden me and the news angers me. Call me
square or lame but I just don't get it.

What happened to the brotherly love? Has the need to
belong become so great that we are willing to kill our
future just to fit in?

Hell I can no longer worry about if my brother's keeping me, cuz I'm too busy worrying about him creeping me.

Has a spot or territory become so prominent that we are willing to sacrifice our freedom just to say "dis my block." Mind you, you don't own the shit in the first place.

But day by day, blood stains the streets and seeps into the sewage of our youth, becoming permanently embedded in their thoughts, transforming into their actions, with no shame.

All we care about is fast money, and our kids can barely speak English correctly, but they know how to cuss or better yet bust.

There's no more us.

When life was simple and the air was sweet. When music was smooth and streets were safe.

Sometimes I hope that when I go to sleep and wake up the next day it would have all been a sick dream.

But I know that day will never come, so all we can do is join hands by the masses and pray til our lungs collapse with sorrow. Praying to get our streets back, praying to get our homes back. Praying to get those days back.

Constantly singing we shall overcome and a change is gonna come till our souls burst.

Tears quenching our thirst.

Hearse after hearse......Bring those days back

...... can we please bring those days back.

The Nerd

He said nice guys like him finish last.

And yeah I can see where that would be true.

After all he does carry a pocket calculator and protractor clipped to his belt.

But some of us women don't know a good man when we see one.

And yes I said it.

We have this whole fictitious illusion or definition of what a real man is, that when one is in our presence we overlook him like he the bell boy or something.

It seems to me like the more dog like the dude is the more we pull to him.

Mesmerized by his roughness and bluntness.

We stand by while he fucks with other women waiting for him to bring her essence to our place, her sweetness invading our space, her pussy juices smeared all over his face and we kiss him.

But there stands alone Mr. Okie Dok.

With the dork-ish of grins on his face.

Just waiting for the right woman to come along so that he can give her his all.

Captured by her beauty and unidentified power.

All he wants to do his shower her with love and life and make her feel that way she wants to feel even if it's in a corny manner

But naw we don't want that.

He too green and lame is what we say.

So we settle for the dudes who could frankly care less about our existence.

Will drop us with the quickness if we not willing to fit into his world.

Chasing girl after girl heartless and cruel.

But that ignites us for some stupid reason.

Not knowing that we are worth so much more.

Not knowing that we deserve the respect and honor.

Then when we get our feelings hurt we might run to Mr. Okie Dok so he can lick the wounds.

Using po' dude for a free meal.

Then at the end of the night you tell him you're not that into him, but it's not him though.

Bitch please.

But shit, if that aint your type then, who am I to stand in the way?

As for me, I want that nerd known as Mr. Okie Dok.

I get turned on by that smart shit.

Give me the mother fucker that can pick my brain and stimulate my mind with calculations.

You may call him green, but with him I see green.

A dynamic equilibrium type couple moving mountains conquering the impossible.

Making moves and making history by creating traffic signals in the sky for flying cars and shit.

And let's not talk about how many ways we can

calculate our love making.

Every time he sticks his radius into my circumference I have quadruple Vertical Ellipses

The parameter of the bed doesn't sum up to enough square footage so we have to take out Integral Methods to other areas of the 4 dimensional space we call a home. His circular functions are constant and differential.

Mmmm … and the length, width and volume of his cylinder sends my pyramid on an Algebraic seizure ready to straddle his axis.

Our Pythagorean Theorem is like no other.

So while you round here licking the other chick juices off of so called Mr. Right.

Me and Mr. Okie Dok will be making combustion and solving equations even Einstein couldn't figure out.

Eagerly reciprocating each other's oral dissertations.

Finding the square root to the nervous system and formulating a union of our molecules creating our love.

Damn how I love to clean his bifocals.

No I'm not saying that all straight laced cats are dogs and all squares are honest.

I just want y'all ladies to know that rough ain't always right and sometimes green can be good.

Get to know a person and see what they really are about.

Learn to step away from the norm and step outside the box and walk around that bitch.

You might be amazed what ya find on the other side.

The next 3 poems maybe considered graphic. I
have the tendency of writing out of emotion but
I stand by my work.

A Love of Your Own

What you mad at me for? I ain't da one dat said da shit.

You just know that deep down inside you just a trifling bitch.

So now you hatin and faking cuz you too scared to admit.

That there's a lot of envy in ya cuz I'm da one riding his dick.

See I wrote this poem for all you chicks who won't stop and quit.

Too blinded by the past so for the present they just try to omit.

Yeah what y'all had was good, but now it's gone, so stop boo dats it.

Just take it as a loss, pack yo bags and jus split.

But no you don't wanna do dat, and now ya friends done

boost ya up to cause a scene.

So now you playing on my phone like you're the childish age of 16.

See hoe' I know it be you, cuz yo fuck ass breathe with a wheeze.

Then I heard yo sick ass daddy in the back ground with his cough and his sneeze.

But I wasn't gone blast ya out cuz like you I done been down that road before.

So heartbroken and bitter that it's too hard to let go.

But all the Facebook slander is wearing me thin you stupid ho.

Keep requesting me with these fake pages like my ass don't know.

You spell your city the same way in all your locations.

With the capital letters and acronyms in them dumb ass

quotations.

See I wanna wipe yo ass of the planet Earth or at least out the equation.

Just seeing you laid up under a pickup truck would be such an elation.

Or maybe if a piano fell on your head as you walked down the street.

Black and white keys embedded in your brain would make my life complete.

But I ain't gone put my hands on ya cuz I'm too fancy and too meek.

But you keep snoopin and being nosy and you gone find what it is you seek.

I'm speaking this shit for the women who are tired of you petty ass broads.

Y'all be walking around like you got your shyt together

but we know it's just a facade.

It was you who started playing games from the very start.

Now you know I'm lookin for ya so you wanna duck and dodge.

It's y'all dumb ass stupid antics which set us black women so far back.

And it's y'all dumb ass chicken heads that I want to compact.

Or maybe I could just tie you down to a railroad track.

Or I could just frame yo ass by lacing yo apartment with bags of crack.

See I'm furious and just little bit upset right now.

But your home wrecking ways no longer will I allow.

Imma uproot and your evil wickedness with my mental shovel and my humble plow.

The curtains have closed on your stage play so go on ma take a bow.

But there won't be an encore presentation cuz his love don't live with you anymore.

Y'all shit was in the past so get loss, like I told you once before.

We even now boo, so no more trying to settle the scores.

You better back up before I slice yo ass and po salt all in your sores.

No I ain't Billy Bad ass. I aint even a bear.

I'm just protecting my rightful half of he and I's share.

So you can gone head and try to destruct it. Have at it. I dare.

But the drama you may try to bring won't even compare.

Compare to the love he and I share and the faith he has in me.

Our Loyalty and commitment and built up security.

Shawty and nothing you can say or do is gone make me flee.

Cuz I'm a bad mother fudge cake that much you have to agree.

So for y'all ladies who be up in the new chicks lane gone head and find your own zone.

Stop all the fighting, bickering, slander and the playing on the phones.

All that petty shit ain't cute and you just might find yourself all alone.

Get yourself together and grow the hell up and find a love of your own.

This piece almost didn't make the book. I can't really explain why but it was written as a challenge presented by another poet. We both had the same view but different preferences yet the possibility to step on someone's toes was inevitable from either one of our lips. Maybe I was feeling some type of way when I wrote it but it's funny and true if you frequent the poetry scene a lot.

Spit

Show and prove. That should be the poetry Golden Rule.

If you gone spit it you should walk it.

Nuff with all the talk shyt.

How many people can your bark hit.

Personally, I don't dislike poems about how you spit.

If the shoe fit then gone head and wear it.

95

Make me aware of your spit.

Cuz when the curtains are down and the lights come on.

I wanna see if you can own up to that shyt you spit.

I wanna yearn to feel the burn of how deep yo spit get.

I want yo spit to assure me that through any stormy weather, hard time or financial heartache Imma get through it.

I want you to channel your spit through my brain frequencies and cause me to better the inner me.

I want your spit to solve my unsolved mystery.

Right now is not the time for the fakers and floggers because the gloves have come out and I'm throwing them knockers, harder and harder, tryin real hard to dodge ya.... If your spit ain't real.

My life is no game so it's your spit that I'm trying to feel.

Whether it be gift or skill.

When you come to the light, you should already know

what the deal.

Boo keep it real when you step on the stage.

All that part time frontin shyt ain't making the grade.

Hell we all hungry out here and we all trying to get paid.

But if the truth is really in ya then you will never evade.

Spit that power for days.

Cuz you may never know what sacrifices I have made, or that the only thing that will ease my mind is a poetic serenade.

Cuz I've seen poets, who have people in awe and mesmerized at their abilities to spit life in dead tulips and roses, spitting pure hocus pocus thinking no one will notice that they can't speak life in their own self-esteems, or secure their insecurities. Poets be hiding behind floral limericks like no one can see.

And I've seen poets spit knowledge wisdom and new

meaning to the lost women of the world. Spitting self-love with a dove and giving verbal diamonds and pearls. But at the end of their set and they have spit all they can spit, they busy spitting to various chicks tryin to get one to split on their shit.

Now you know you need to quit.

Stop spitting for self-gratification and go out on the streets and begin to witness.

Spit til your word becomes relentless.

Spit so much that your silence makes bodies cringe and…

Spit you way up veins through needles of syringes…

Spit cuz you numero uno in a one man show.

Spit your way to that bridge and prevent that person from letting go.

Spit cuz you're gung ho or spit like you already know.

Spit like the end is near.

Spit with no shred of fear.

Spit til you see clear.

Spit til answers appear.

Just spit.

Spit cuz my mouth dry from telling you how to spit, so now I need yo spit to moisten me up a little bit.

Hell, just spit!

But when you spit... That shyt better stick.

Like a Saturated wad of paper on the wall that shyt better stick.

Like thick ass oatmeal or cheese grits that shyt better stick.

Like sweaty ass nuts to a thigh, that shyt better stick.

Like Hillary Clinton during her baby daddy infidelity scandal, that shyt better stick.

Like a black man felony record, that shyt better stick.

Like a lace front on them edges, that shyt better stick.

Like them dentures and poly grip that shyt better stick.

Like that birth control patch you wear on yo back, that shyt better stick.

For when you spit, you better show and prove.

Hell fuck it, cuz that is the Poetry Golden Rule.

Period, point blank, simple and legit.

Don't spit that shit if you can't walk that shyt!

A Fifth of Loyalty

You're so vain.

I bet you think this poem is about you.

I mean well it kinda is but not in a heartfelt sense.

More like an I hate your existence cuz you give me hemorrhoids type sense.

You weren't worthy of my lung capacity, so I picked up the pen.

And I started writing I hate you I hate you over and over again.

But then it clicked that you could probably make me a masterpiece.

Nothing but 10's at the stage poetry slam kinda piece.

An HBO Def Poetry Jam kinda piece.

Mother fucker you don't know who the fuck I am, I'm going ham kinda piece.

See there comes a time in life when a woman just wants to vent to the 1st mother fucker that will hear.

So I Thank y'all for paying your cover charge, cuz this you all must hear.

Everything ain't always as beautiful as it may appear.

Cuz there's a lot fuck shyt and back stabbing going on round here.

See there's this bitch, who thinks I give two fucks of a shyt.

Bout some shyt that she heard but wasn't woman enough to step to me wit.

Do you think I give a fuck if he hit it and quit it.

Hell with the looks of yo ass then yo face, I'd probably hit it and split.

But that's not my concern.

And hopefully a good lesson is what you learned.

That all you can do is get fucked from a nigga that ain't "yerns."

And speaking of niggas. Let me tell you how this lil so and so had the nerve to try me.

Oh he thought that cuz he put the dick down that he could grab my car keys.

Nigga my name's on that registration, and I'm the one that pay that high ass car fee.

So unless yo ass paying that car note I suggest you get ta walken.

Oh no I ain't done. I got a whole lotta motha fukas dat done pissed me off.

You show folk nuthin but love but all they wanna do is fuck you raw.

See I ain't graduate from the school of the hard knocks and I don't live by the law.

I believe in playing the cards I was dealt and hopefully in the end they were the luck of the draw.

Even in my family that prays there's blasphemy that goes on day to day.

They'll talk behind yo back and ke ke ke all up in yo face.

Be all up in the Lord's house, shouting for glory and giving him praise.

But let you fall on hard times, see how many of them will give you a place to stay.

Folk at my job will snitch on you every the chance they get.

They too cheap to fire yo ass so they aggravate cha hoping you will quit.

I guess that's the price you pay when you're not ridin the bosses dick.

Some of them mother fuckers be kissin ass so much I can smell the shyt on their lips.

Man I'm tired of writing about these fuckers cuz the shyt will never end.

And I refuse to live my life wondering how many people will fuck me over as a friend.

A lot of times that shyt hurt and I ain't about to stand here and front or pretend.

That's why I always keep super glue on standby in case

my shattered heart I would ever have to mend.

Thank you for reading, now let's finish this book off on a lighter note!

Do you know her?

Have you ever met a woman that was burnt out.

Heart so heavy, not even God had the strength to lift her.

Mentally worn and emotionally torn from life's falsified pickups and guaranteed let downs.

Nothing but thick dark gray clouds hovering over her every step.

Disappointed with the hand she was dealt, she's ready to throw in the towel.

For the life of her she can't seem to wrap her brain around the error of her ways.

Constantly retracing her life's step, trying to see which path she went down which was labeled "Wrong Turn"

107

Yearning to extinguish the burn that scorched her heart.

She doesn't know who she can trust.

Family, friends, lovers and religion let her down a long time ago.

So now she's bitter.

Looking and lurking lustfully for the love she may never find.

Do you know her?

Shattered remnants of a time that use to be plaguing her thoughts.

There was a time when she felt free and secure from the notions of this wicked earth.

Do you know her?

Anxiously waiting for someone to show her that her life was not created in vain.

That she was not birthed through a sacred canal just to live in shame.

Do you know her?

She regrets believing every promise once fed to her, because for one reason after another it was broken. Just like

her heart which is now broken. Suicidal thoughts and attempts go unspoken.

Do you know her?

Trying with every shred of strength she possesses to climb to the top and stay there, but an unforeseen gust knocks her back down every time.

No crimes has she ever committed, but yet and still she is spiritually, mentally and emotionally incarcerated.

Do you know her?

Because I know her.

I see her every day standing at the bus stop waiting for that next 11:45 shuttle to take her to a better beginning. But she is only hit with the reality that the fare she just paid is only going to drop her off at her daily 8 to 12 not 8 to 5 ritual because her hours were cut months ago. So although her bills may not have changed her cash flow has. So she robs Peter to pay Paul only to get a late night phone call from Jamal cuz he wanna get his meat wet. And she knows that she needs some of his pay check so she feels that her best bet is to let dat nigga creep in them sheets, cuz after all she and her kids gotta eat.

I see her every day, sitting bedside by her ailing child. Praying countless prayers and shedding endless tears. Asking God why her child was not given the same childhood as the average. Eagerly watching as the nurses accurately refill every dosage of that make you feel better serum in the syringe. Wishing one needle stick after the next will be the last and the last will be the one that makes her child whole. For not long ago she was given that heart wrenching bad news that her child didn't have long to go. So she grips her child's hand and places gentle motherly kisses on the back of their hand. Putting it in the Lord's hands.

I see her every day rocking away in her rocking chair on her cluttered front porch. With nothing but her old hound dog by her side this is the only family she has. Her husband left her many years ago for a pretty young thang from around the way. She rocks away staring bitterly out to the world. No one sees her hurt. On the exterior all that is shown to man is an old wrinkled hateful bag. But she cries inside. She cries knowing that she did all she could as a wife. But now she finds herself torn and alone.

We see that burnt out woman every day. All races, shapes, ages and beliefs she exists. Whether you

choose to accept it, she is here. But now is not the time
to have pity on her, but to lend her your ear. Assure her
that she is not in this fight alone. Some say trouble don't
last always but who is to be for certain. Until you have
taken at least one step in her shoes, you may never know
what she has to go through. A lot of women are not
bitches because they want to be. But life has had a
strong hold on them so tight, they couldn't break loose
to see what happiness felt like. So now they may be
untrusting and unforgiving, skeptical and unwilling.
Don't be so quick to turn the other cheek.

Help that lady with all them bags as she walks
down the street, call for help if you hear or see a woman
getting beat, and ladies don't think for one moment that
her same shoes can't be placed on your feet.

So if you have ever met a woman that you
thought to be burned out if all you can offer is

112

conversation, your simple words of encouragement may just be the perfect prescription to help her out.

I know I have given you all a lot to take in, so I want to keep my last piece short and to the point. I wrote this piece at a time where I was reaching to connect. I got the opportunity to participate in a rally against racism with the YWCA and this piece came from that reach. I ended up calling a 5th grade class up front and recited the poem to them and all of Uptown Charlotte. I felt calmness all over me. I walked to the bus terminal and a guy came up to me and said he saw what I did and thanked me. I was numb with gratitude. Thank you for reading and be great!

Inspirational Piece

Do it because they don't expect you to.

Do it as proof that you're better than you.

Relinquish your fear and work like you breathe.

Life is mean.

And so are the people who walk with it.

Refocus your vision and protect your image.

If you're truly unapologetic don't explain.

Let them think what they're gonna think

There are far greater dimensions of this world to be

stuck in a small sector.

Boxed in puppets beginning to fester in desperate need

of curbside service.

Know your purpose.

In life it's good versus the ways of the world.

You can either go in the direction of destruction and

greed.

Or Build empires from your thoughts and make gold

with all the knowledge you seek.

No shame in being unique.

You're just a trend setta, go getta, only wanting betta.

You are not your mistakes. Your destiny should be worth your chase.

Adjust your focus, always being willing to listen and do whatever it takes.

No matter what the obstacle may be keep doing it.

No matter how far-fetched that idea may seem, keep pursuing it.

No matter how big or wide the mountain may be still move it.

Your fate should be your ultimate desire.

And the Can'ts and ain'ts will only inspire.

Don't compromise your character and keep your dignity intact.

Learn to be slow to speak and not so quick to react.

For the many blessings that have been bestowed upon

you, make sure you give those blessings back.

And if there's anyone around that feels they can't do it,

just pick up their slack, and haul it on your back and

keep your track.

Don't let anyone deprive you of the things you know you

could do

The impossible is just a possibility that your will can

renew.

Learn to step out on faith and put your fear to the side.

Begin to bury all the doubt and let your strength be your

guide.

With just hunger and determination you can only

prevail.

So you can sit back and relax and watch your future

unveil.

KIAFLOW.COM

Thank you for Going with The Flow!

Made in the USA
Columbia, SC
10 April 2022

58759469R00065